How We Saved the City

Cover art used with permission of the artists:
Tom Bubul
Cybele Collins
Jo Dery
Jungil Hong
Xander Marro
James McShane
Mike Taylor

First Edition, January 2012

Library of Congress Cataloging-in-Publication Data
Schapira, Kate 1979-
How We Saved The City /
poems by Kate Schapira
ISBN 978-0-9840285-0-4 (Paperback)

Stockport **Flats** 2012

1120 East Martin Luther King Jr. Street Ithaca, NY 14850 (607) 272-1630

www.stockportflats.org

How We Saved the City

poems

Kate Schapira

CONTENTS

Prologue: Magical Urbanism

I was walking home when a glow caught my eye: the mulch around a municipal tree was burning. Got down to scrape it out and found there was more underneath than I thought. Two men walking the other direction saw and stopped to help me, using a corner of loose brick. How I could have reacted whitely while we were squatted down getting the last embers; their black stopping; a spare thought early at night; we dusted our hands off, a line in my head captured the little glows: *The evening was alive with first responders*, already turning it. Respective cities closed over us again.

Dispatches from the Interior

Sugarbook

a misreading

the old omens had left abruptly
circumstances that made people human

the house strewn practically overnight, benevolent
leftovers in plastic, plastic down from the crags

gauze aided by a description of gauze

The white city pearled in reflections from dirty water. Cupolas and belfries scaled one another like pairs or quatrains of mating bugs, spiracled for their own breathing room only. By morning, the woman crouched in a condemned doorway had gained a urinary tract infection and varicose veins. Fat drops.

As if upward were a foregone conclusion, as if clean new dwellers would automatically come striding as soon as clean new dwellings were prepared for them. This changed to become, As soon as they will have stood ceremonially empty ...

The harpies' building used to be higher and more in keeping. They stuck there, ensconced without capitals. They waited for the siege engines, soft black eyes like flesh under missing skin in their cultural faces.

The old fell in droves invisible from the river walkways. No one was certain except the planners, who were very certain. In a former building, two boys sorted a career's worth of Last Wills and Testaments. Offices stained and milky where furniture had been.

A mooring ready every few days, they bumbled over the leaf of the city limits, bramble leaf with white underside, which grows without grounds. It's not that it's forgotten, but who's forgotten it. An anthem, or a motive. The loaves rose and rose as if implicit and time bent around them.

The woman who wanted to be a harpy without brass claws or dead bodies probed a cake recipe instead, considered the pockets of mini-meaning created by the city's people and wondered if these were real or not, or just railings

with no hint of what was in the sky

the cherubic facets of the new
edifices, their fine-grained gleam

Street Value

Businesses open and close luxuriously, stretch and capitulate like summer morning. Giving directions, we forget our reasons. Place to park, spend or dawdle in spending dandles us on its stone bosom, tax breaks like a high heel, splash of fallen sandwich tomato or berry birdshit on a broad granite lip. Linen and Lycra fountain through, a plashing spangled with pennies. Someone must know where they go.

{- You must follow me! <giggles> If you don't follow me <giggles> you will be shot in the back!}

Natural manual for new desire in the kind of people. Images of angels bless the ravioli fabricator now. Rich sample of credit, loose balloon of credence, fits itself to the sensory surface. Steel skin, plaster stone, plastic and drywall and foam, open their starlet eyes. Hopefully,

{- How big is that shit? Does that shit bite?}

the color of fruit. The color of shells. The color of lipstick. The color of nodding. The color of liquids. The color of leather. Although no growth permits between the stones it's greenly reminiscent to encourage, antiqued to authenticate, inlaid here, pregnant with weekend meaning. When value's social what it touches is itself, all the whole meeting

{-Angel, in your room, now!}

coaxed here. But don't come from here. But come here to live, or remain profuse in anticipation, or never intended. Wishes overflow as they vanish. Handholders' gender habits high and narrow as the unveiling of a building, oilslick on undertone, eyelash coffee, imported. A static shock to stand close to. Silky cheese drapes the tongue, all the way from.

{- That's nasty, yo, that shit's nasty!}

The old country of beautiful presentation dangles invitingly, wiped down by time. "Memento mori" doesn't mean remember the dead, it means remember *you* will die, which is why the city builds an invitation to what accumulates. Towers fake-stencil reminders on the clouds, fake-ice the lines, heavily produce.

{- Shut up!
 - No! Lalalalalala ...}

Panic or calculation that can take away can also replace. But it won't be the same or the weave before. For that the city needs imports, bouquet occasions carefully managed. If a glow adheres as you pass through the folding doors, you may be a desirable component of the lacelike, complex pushing. Or you may throw yourself back like a fish from the actual river.

{-That's what they did to me! And that's what they're gonna do to you, if you keep stealing shit!}

As a loving investment ingredient, softness shines under bone. Ingenuous eye-meeting: if you don't make it, imagine it. Pastry convolutions harmonize with slabbed surfaces, draped and pinned and thumbed over. Dreamed-up migration, the street next day all fronts. In the possible day, on the way to somewhere less enthused. In the avuncular night, stubbed out on a sidewalk table. You have to hand it to them.

Revolving Fund

... as a name in concrete is to memory as ...
fingertip is to silence ... recent
clandestine ... where the record of changes is not
in common use ... *I have never felt more* ... Newcomers
may well ... prised, even remembering they've never
seen what ... before. To ensure that ... *safe and comfortable*
and to maintain ... my all ... and successfully. *Enter*
three pieces; give them five ends; hedge out;
... Countenanced. Is my face ... All behind us; behind *creative*
people who enrich ... but worth their corner.
For wh ... noticeable we ... mercy in the form
of color, of shoring up,

... of scraping to be done will
... ment, flush or suffusion of this
neighb ... it needs: *Put in your goods, keep*
them well handled,

in swirls ... *this seemingly class-conscious* ... to be
mitred, praised, culturally ... inhabited ... longer ... follows

conflict that has apparently ... trying to emulate
minutes of this meeting ... bett ... keep details
important. As ... uable as real
gives out its color in a similar manner. Primary,
a particul ... *little idea* ... of dream, promontory
from which however little else is visible ...

Propped on a piece of dry rot and two overturned
buckets: PLEASE USE SIDE ENTRANCE and two
men lean over it, smoking also, ... direction ... uplif ... feeling,
showplace, to be shown, to ... places ... *I came*
in with a respect ... brewing ...

While ... ing on with it, two women smoke
together and tap on the steps. Look coolly. It's on ... side,
on either ... of them, the ratty siding ... scrapes ...
make an echo. Genie Lift in the back yard

shines and contracts to make for you ... rection
of any protocol ... up, upward, up and coming, unkinking
associations by use of *a sufficient quantity of purple*
archil ... piece of green copperas the size ... one ounce of
bluestone of vitriol ... Liquescence ... asset,

acidulate, names of chemicals change ... and expiration
date for each revo ... of doorknob or hinge ... where change
comes in, ... *more dismissive than cruel.* Pour
and stir motives into the sur ... fix ... circus colors, service
leak, bought up and stained ... rfeit as we can imagine. Mordants ...

dyes last, ... tangible ... the change
readily imparted by the following simple process, ... how
much better motives are under ... how much we've ... *It will*
be understood how ... an aim ... or not the houses empty, voices
heard ... *It is with much regret that I have lost ...*

older undercoat ... flat, as if choral,
but shallowly. *This finishes them*. ... questionably
... a position to question. ... *a fine gloss*.

This vat continues to be
good until exhausted, hence "revolving" for whi ...
used also ... guards set over new
cement in folding chairs to prevent a few
blocks away where names bite into the bottom of lampp ...

to make people feel safe ... paint ... *no*
confidence ... a show of feeling ... a *rich fabric* ...

Endowed

Graft: first heard: slip, branch, gash, growth.

(Zoning; permits; things to do. Contractors; sewage; things to do. Demolition. Things. Design, design, to do. More permits. And the roads and walks that lead to be made smooth.)

Lay your hand to the switch and light comes
on. How to better it. Brick inlay
angled, storefronts regaled, little parks,
benches, street and other names.

Saints' parks: saints are givers. Sometimes
exclusively. Often dramatically. What they
get and don't forget. A poor
match, maybe, to light candles.

(Water; things to do; electricity. Roofing, things to do. Pipes for heat, pipes for water, pipes for things. State of the lamppost art to do. Four men carrying an enormous pane of glass down the street perfectly shows it.)

Code in doubt but the building up
to it. Elsewhere within
the limits (within limits?) statues
have risen, bridges been
repaired, organizations fostered, libraries
nursed, shells puffed full. Assailed

by a whiff of
pulp protection
lump the population

identify one lack
among many, call it a need. To do
something. Don't know
much is protection. Let's
not forget binding,

(Things to do: select.)

bring in what needs deciding.
Lay your hand to the switch.
It expands talking
traffic, talking in circles
carefully laid.

(Things toilets to order, do countertops.)

What will they eat and wear
where will they shit and talk
whom will they not see. Shipment
of promise to pick up or drop
this statue of a benefactor,

(Awnings to go up. To do. Heating to install, and A/C. Things to do; coming soon; things to do.)

this attraction. Ghost trap for
people who aren't yet there.
Strenuous. Pre-use. In mind
contracted. It's just
like doing what you can
for the city. The name

(Staff to hire. Heating to pay, things to do, or A/C. Carpet to cut and lay and things. Curtains. To do lightbulbs; more advertising is never enough to do things. Front desks.)

a mighty yet gentle influence you'll prove it.

(Sidewalks swept. Streets salted. Garbage emptied. Streets sanded. Sand swept. Streets emptied.)

Insulate veins with news that
features your name. Roll earplugs. Paper
compartments. Blot grease. No one
can say you've done nothing. Needs
to become. Whose once they're here

means something
entirely: remarkable, protected,
or all alike. Whose notice escaped you.

(All this has been a map to do with each its correspondence.)

St. Joseph's halo of star-shaped green and pink
Christmas lights: lay your hand to the switch.

The object of my dream is to skyline as the center is to a column of air

featuring,
A., *an activist/agitator*
The flying boy, *a flying boy*

In the municipal river the reflection of a tree blocks the reflection of the sun as A. moves her head sideways, although she isn't looking at either the real tree or the real sun

looking at

decisive nature in the water leads to murals on the underpass as industry in the water incites the rehabilitation of green weeds into the bright future. Enflamed under the working sun that can't be seen past the protection of civic trees, A. has something to say to the flying boy of wary faces
in the city in
the way they should go
furthering their authentic creases
wanting what's best for them.

In the exemplary tale, residents and passers-through change what they mean. Migrations of wealth pass themselves off as sun and water

apple coating
bright mural government
beginning to turn
on enormous pivots, generally or privately speaking. With effort A. transmutes laryngitis into sound, movement

coming into view

forcing blood to her surface to change her as she crosses, implanting a businesslike
looseness at the
crux of her limbs,
her boxcar climbs
the crest rattletrap echoing
deep runnels the sound of skyline
possible as spires or centers

pulls her lip under to make a vacancy, her skeleton of I-beams up. A tiny dinner table and chairs, longlimbed in metal, wedded to a Core 10 horizontal. Who could have put it there?

Look for thunder in the scrubland that reads as
vacant lots
pale strangers far from home. Robbing her own house, A. changes as crosses, looks wildly for her keys and other bag on public transit before realizing she didn't bring them. Dreams
with multiple
axles thundering over
event coordination
apple-juggling dilettante
dreaming the wrong address, the tips

of which are catching on fire, no thanks to the sun's weak focus. If it could keep on task and not splinter in the surfaces. "How are you doing with mob psychology?" the flying boy asks A.
reddened tip of her nose protruding through her hands
his penis and undescended
testicles bobbing solemnly
but is he serious?

"If people need to know or only knew or knew more already or need—what they need—"
Tooth and untooth

missions or giants kneeling awkwardly and with great responsibility. Noon waves on the margin of the neighborhood. Forgets her mission in fear. Misdirected projections, examples, recriminations,
pale strangers
offering
high platforms.

She feels her throat grow used to the sight.

His skin and hair smell like a bottle rocket. Heated armpits. Seats to fill. Fraying a hole of disapproval in her skyscraper, skyscraper's reflection in the windows of a nearby scraper and a sky that's all window. Short snags or thickenings of progress,

short shakes no
great as an agitator

ear untuned for
earnest or gibing
inspection for orthodoxy: a form of safety. Her dreams don't object to goading the horizon or standing in the way. Far from it. She makes notes, smells air. Schematics gray and stray

harassment tactics
flash hope warnings
wrong sources for voices:

Gear-like rim or center valorizes iron, the work of the workers, the plight of the metal
elaborates
amplifies
claws A.'s fatigue. Becomes more ornate than mirrors, more fraught than associations,

more stigmatized than apples

striking
highly damaging
considerable damage.

The middle of the action working fast. She wants to be in it. To be a cause, to cause, not ease, belonging, not belonging, passing through, not passing through. Throwing the switch. Watching the street. These things take time. He wobbles toward the river.

Loyalties other than those
leave gifts or sacrifices—A. finding
her back bent
double is not enough.
Her skyline flickers. Before she knows
agreement lurches

she stretches out her hand. Appeal leaves all
behind, panting up, blunt wings
shadow against
the stacks like smoke.

A Far Cry

Surrender the key to its hooks. Furrows of bright air, stereo windows open at the intersection. Crane dangling red bait. Dry country under the ocean where apples bloom incessantly. Shirt in layers of Caribbean green leads to just thinking about it, door printed in the air. Magnetic tape glitters in trees, caught. Pretense of access, odor of cooking never places it at the center but always somewhere. Airfish float so sweetly among. Bait blows high.

Flame-retardant monsters differ in different countries; different countries are different things at times; the country under the ocean always is, from here. A luminous parade winds through it. The color of travel-agent oceans, of postcards. Dear country with a brown sand floor how do I enter you. Dear living in the country of found. I can't wake up today and find myself somewhere. Dear uneven ink.

Always underwater, in the air, trees, never transplanted. Opens with a key the size of the one in the window. Maybe they'll catch an airfish. Six tables and five gray men: one bald head and glasses. One hat and tattoo blurring. One glasses and beard. One head pillowed on his arms. One alert to a magazine. The van says, "Ocean Options," like a talking dolphin. Steel surfaces, like a dolphin, for easy cleaning.

Birds come back to red against blue. Garland of shame, boxwood and stinging cedar. To show that as a country we have customs. Fishy smell of cleaning fluids, readiness to improve, to be like difference. People invent a car that goes under the ocean to show. The gift of walls makes them like birds. Makes birds like airfish: the grinning patch, its drawbacks, cost of materials.

Make your sure safe. Against the bright sky. Don't seek that blessing. Don't reach across the counter in the foreground. It will be denied to you, like something different. Tear up cheap carpet at the thought of mold. Scrub the dolphin with a toothbrush. Get at grease and dead skin, the apple trees are gearing up, white blossom will stand out, red fruit, be ready, ready, away from the center. Nothing could be further.

Weird Math I

+ dishes by hand – no dishpan, inefficient + organic lettuce and carrots + she smiles at me – down the disposal – outside my neighborhood (– I make my paper copies – their chemicals) + health-food dish soap – in the brick zombies of my friends' old home (– driving to get them – don't know who picked them – for the chain store – trucked them) – lights on in the kitchen – on North Main Street – at Eagle Square – (the honor system + lingering) – in plaza geometry – good edible particles – uncertain goya and eggplant + dishwasher we don't use – driving distances – filling with swampy runoff – mosquito larva – bleaching it =

The curve, also, of responsible eating; the heart of heat; a swab of feeling guilty, cold against; refuge in columns. That one could neutralize or cancel the other out. Math takes many forms: installment plans, first last and security, name earrings, art in the blood, dogs, speculative development, dimensions of banners, two or three to a bed, accounts, changes of dressing per day, acreage, penny-pinching, reciprocal favors, head counts, square screen inches.

Which was made. Which just grew. A cloud falls on thinking, a math that precipitates, crystallizes into the purity of inaction above the branded smokestack, factory air, stiller and stiller until the snow comes. If sorry doesn't count, guilt is not disinfectant, just cold. Old calipers from our measuring days, ourselves as engines humming looms, the looming floss. Architecture chambered for comparison releases to the operation each component, each human bead and wire responsible for its own turning.

Distributive. Guilt is weird math because it attempts to resolve, it obscures the heart till I can't think where it's gone. Property. The same to both sides as if I hadn't done anything, as if balancing. Separates. Cities superscripted, motions between them rimmed in glass. Openings between them like the mouths of birds. Like the difference between the mouths of birds and their nests.

The Love of Freak Millways and Tango Wax

I don't know, I fooled around with it once. Began to think the Kat is a girl—even drew up some strips with her being pregnant. It wasn't the Kat any longer ... Then I realized Krazy was something like a sprite, an elf. They have no sex. So that Kat can't be a he or a she. The Kat's a spirit—a pixie—free to butt into anything. Don't you think so?

- George Herriman

In the study of touch, scratched skin picks out from under nails like worm turds in summer. Unbend a skin of touches all the way back to the elbow, first meeting, first dry plane tree leaves overheard, dirty hair, someone gets up, adjusts the focus, dust descends like a rain of congratulations, the movie starts.

Setting Up

Duct tape?

Check.

Tails?

Check.

Beer cups from the benefit?

Check, but next time we should use the rewashable cups.

Okay. Plastic bags?

Um—negative on the plastic bags. Any corner stores around here?

There's the So-No-Co.

I'll check their dumpster. Are we missing anything else? What about the feather masks?

I thought you said the rhinestone masks.

No, the feather masks to go with the tails.

Oh.

It's okay, honey, we can go up with the rhinestone masks.

I could've sworn you said—

Don't worry about it, let's just make sure we have everything else. Burned-out glow sticks?

Check.

Extension cord?

Check.

Soldering iron?

Check.

Good. Great. Fine. I'll go check the dumpster and meet you at the construction site in twenty minutes. Wait, what about the mistletoe?

We decided not to use the mistletoe.

The use of clothes in dreaming

They* are on blankets in the burned house, the Herriman quote cross-stitched above their bed-corner, its nail tucked into the nail-hole made before they were born, could be, mold-poured. Sometimes Tango forgets what used to be made here. Recasts the thought: what people used to make here. Culpable material. Keeping grammar ethical is so hard that Tango wonders if they are not the spirits of the city after all. Clutches Freak's sleeping knots—rats'-nests, elf-locks. When they took each other on, Tango hadn't known what the bones of the head and the hand entail, or that money would start spilling into the city from all sides, not soaking in but buoying up their pallet against its wishes. They try to think. How look at it? Tango thinks hard, rubbing wrists where the harness bound them to overpass chain-link, ridges where the swiss seat** cut in. Cars rushing under like the poisonous universe at the height of ownership. By siren time, they were gone, two lovers to the burned house of temporary safety. Sought or unsought, small stitches between air and midair. Tango wants new ways to think about it, wants to scrap, but nothing is worth destroying. Share everything they save: Freak's facebolts belong to both although Tango has no holes for them. Pants, sweatshirts, the same lucky size, a find is a find.***

*** In an alternate love Freak is smaller, so all clothes have to be let in. And let out. And in, with many pricked fingers, two sets of seams drawn in Sharpie to make alterations easier. Each multiple. Along the rib a web of holes and stitches. If it was me, Tango thinks into the version, I'd wear stuff big, feeling like a spider trapped in its own making in the burned corner. And in this love, this happens.

** A real name for an arrangement of bonds.

* In sharing they left the cult of autonomy, even pronouns: how can you offer anything to your partner, your mate, the only other you're not other than? Freak would be happy to change their method of referral if Tango could come up with anything better.

Branded* living

*The reek of burned hair and singed flesh, the squeals, the loosened bowels, the fellowship of suffering, something, together, what makes us members is the smell, the share, our share of suffering, the corral, the state of it.

Freak is printing an assembly of body parts that all fit together so nicely. All nest, finger muscles sheathing pads that lock squeegee and bone, a stretched tympanic membrane. Final color like a long wet whistle spatters over two Freakish hands. Layers over layers of dirty music, inefficient music, to Freak as bird song, true sound of what surrounds them. All motions produce beauty and protest, motions practice what motions preach, the gender of the future's unsurprisingly hollow bones. The final layer will emulate the empty window but in the red of promise, not the red of demolition. What demolition leaves as its ghost, no chemical depression, approaches flight as music, as pinions.

Used razor?

Check.

Armpits?

Check.

The cardboard bats with riveted wing joints?

Check.

Scrutiny?

Check.

Tango don't ever leave me. Don't ever say you only loved my augmentations.

I might die or something.

That would be okay as long as you didn't *leave* me. I mean you wouldn't be leaving *me*. You know that drawing of all the pigeons and squirrels and rats I did converging on the condos? I'm starting to understand how the condos feel. Like there's a yellow light in each of these empties. And I don't like it.

I promise I will never say I only loved your agenda.

Maybe I'm thinking about it too much.

Did you mean yellow like, "Slow down?"

They live to be forced out. Laid out, spread on the floor, pinned with pins, their next project a giant future skin. Parachute nylon. Linings of free-box coats. Tissue paper to be the weak link. If the codes come down on them, they'll have to roll it all up, carry it out in the night. Freak makes food and lays a bowl in front of the curvature, crouched thighs in dirty long johns, sewing a holder for the support pole by hand. Fingers extend into the seam like the limb bones of an early flying creature. Tango turns, all those joints and extensions recalibrate. Accommodate.* Getting naked on the project. Tango does not move from a crouch the whole time Freak stoops over, grabbing, pulling hair, an orchestration of insertions and bites.

* "Everybody has a mouth and an asshole," Freak says to people who want to know what they *do*, careful not to spill the food.

You ready? Got your brace on?

I'm ready.

Can you get that arm a little higher?

Better?

Perfect. Tell me if I make it too—

That's a little tight.

I don't want you to fall.

I have the swiss seat.

I know, but—

What?

There's a lot of cars down there.

Do the other wrist.

In plaid boxers and leotard. In cape and nipples. Honey.* Crystal strands like childhood amber, tree sap that matted and stuck to hoard. Then it's come in and wash up. Now it's hang, hand over the keys. The worst they could be doing in the cave of wonders they say "ours" about. Their refuge in time of water. Cook dumpster salvage on a camp stove, hang fabrics, experiment with knots, rehearse, lick, argue, bend each other over, cry tears of disobedient sinew, read the fine real estate print with fists shaking. It is their where. Their here. Tributary of a long block, once seedy, before that even stately. Empty of industry the smell of burning flattens nasal passages. Duck and cover the weedy backlot, landslip, sagging fence. Shored up, like a monster helping.

*An acceptable endearment.

Humble is the key to setting out

We have to demonstrate it, or what's the point?

But make it fun. So people will watch. Not—

They'll watch even more if we make fools of ourselves.

I don't know if I can do it.

We'll be joined. In the public eye. The mind. We have to show that like, it's voluntary. That we *live* this way because, because—

I wish we could just be us and send ripples out.

But you said you were committed to performing. That's what you said. To living a publicly gender-free life and showing solidarity with anyone who tries, I mean somebody tries to turn them into a ghost. That's exactly what you said.

It's the foolishness.

Dignity is too—it's for people who can afford to have everything backwards and feel *sad* about the *passing* of things instead of getting out there and getting naked—

I know, it's just—it feels so desperate.

We *are*. It's our survival too. For people to do what they want, you know, not even what *we* tell them. It's exactly what you said. I mean, *I'm* desperate.

Freak's hemming a pair of found pants washed out in the downspout. Thread runs black on black setting the pants an example: as radiant as they are true to themselves. Freak props a book, one painted big toenail in the gutter, *The Place at the End of the World.* Complicated black and white butterfly. Freak thinks, "An angel abroad and a devil at home." I'm a butterfly abroad and a unicorn at home. Dog abroad and a sermon at home. Waves of creation form around Freak's body, lapping out like odor across the floor. Not just Freak, but everybody Freak knows. Not just everybody Freak knows, but everybody.

The art of braiding from underneath

The outline for the hang is silver and can travel up blood: Tango, legs cramping around a stanchion, places all four strands in daylight and an orange helmet no one sees too closely. Sweating and indeterminate, Tango, suspended. A four-strand braid is not like a three-strand braid: you do it in installments and have time to imagine you recognize parts: the fingers are not automatic. Trumped up, Tango sweats, attaches what will later swing, needles cuffed for safekeeping. The strew, the sear, of perspiration, strands twitched out by gravity. What Tango, setting up, can see by looking down.

They are deep in territory. Because of this, almost without thinking, distance accumulates between cats and the curb, between recycle bins and the curb, between loose bags and the curb. Fragments of love notes. Curb bites into worn soles of found shoes. Steeped in recognition before they speak, they think. Fan spins in the breeze without being plugged in, without drawing on.* Hair stiffens into spikes with homemade mud. The ordinary run of things is the mill: it keeps where going is grinding. Held in common, last level of color a scatter like flying fish roe. Insistence its own eardrum.

* They will say they had no way of knowing.

Showing out

To do this right, we should run Narragansett Electric through my veins. Or be horse cops or something. This is so piddly—all this fabric.

But look, if you put a pencil eraser in the middle and twist it ... see ...

It radiates.

It gathers and radiates. And if you start another one here, right outside the tent—

And another one—

If you imagine another one—

If enough people gather around them and radiate utopia—

—Then eventually all the utopias will join to form.

Mine, yours, each person's.

Each of us is radiant.

The world spreads out from each of us.

Put yourself at the center of utopia!

Put everyone else at the center of utopia!

The ripples will ripple out and touch each other—

—Like this.

What we do is the center.

The start.

The point from which everything shines, everything gains on us—

—Like this.

Audience that responds like a charm when called. "Eeewww," Freak sings the next day, hands curled outside the blanket. "Indoor performances are too collectible. Let's never do that again." Light slides down the outside of last night's glass. It starts a fight anyway, because what's necessary is not clear and what's clear is not original—Tango means "organic"—and what's organic is not always available. Perfect overpass, climbable-to; perfect rain dance, electricity dance, migration dance; pure attempt to create affordable housing out of the plastic bags that catch in trees. But people don't stay warned, don't respond to indignation or rescue easy. Lymph and bile pool around their encounters. Needles upright, needles everywhere, needles with blue or orange comet tails in floor cracks, attaching themselves to magnets, turning up in a sleeve. Freak breaks more than two trying, with the floorboards, to push them up through too much cloth. It becomes flea season. This after puncturing a thumbnail once.

Picking at clogged pores on hairy legs, image dominates feeling. Wealth of hair, a welter. Attic swelter. The dominant method of presentation of matter is to act, their best foot forward of four. In this heat, the dogs bark yet this is not the time for shelter.

Black dust, decaying rubber of the roof surround, on everything. Its grime is pure. Tango thinks, maybe this year we'll use less water, be the two dirtiest ... maybe next year ... It's raining, the buckets are out. Under gaps. In gaps. A leaded-glass, drooling sky. Wash water. Don't stay out late, don't travel. Door propped open with a jar of pennies (found). With stage fire. With an old, folded shirt pattern, wedged yellow under the crack. Stop the bleeding, buccaneers, with a handful of webs and keep firing. Stop the burns with a scrip of clay.

Days too wet to salvage, they eat post-dated Saltines and do week-old crosswords from the laundromat before grinding them into papier-mache horns and gauntlets and protuberances, answers inked sometimes wholly or partly in. Matted heads meeting while the leaded daylight lasts.*

*Outdoor fireworks'** dull crumps outdo each other in thick mock-orange light, false sky, invisible from any point in the city. Only the sound, like heat, travels.

Survival* value

*Distinguishes a legend with urbanity.**
**Grace: a bow to the inevitable. Bowing out casts itself as further developments out on the ice of summer likelihood. That is: thin. A blister rises in logic. Everything that was comforting is not, now. Even recycle bins pattern an arched, inadequate back, removed from luck. Will fill with snow when the condos are long built. Categories crouch down or pee in the burned corner formed by wall and gravel drift. Grain ergot and old stone. Freak says, "We of the city believe," and Tango says, "Can you go to sleep?" "How can I go to sleep?" "Well, can *I* sleep?" Litter of seams around, trimmed, blankets knot in the middle of a knot, whole habitation spreads in the wrinkles they prescribe. The moment giving no satisfaction but fights.

Be true.

But I can't be true just to you.

Tell me again what the greatest adventure is.

Utopia is the greatest adventure.

But isn't the greatest adventure always in the future?

No, you know, people think that ...

But isn't utopia what people think?

There's less to this than they planned: hanging. Someone really looking for them could find them. Turning hurts to be clearly seen using only available light. More interested in results, they climb down into the small hours.

**Fireworks

Lip-biting. Renewal. Wastage, fizzle, finger potentially blown off. Shoulder-biting one's opposite number, for, privy to, provided for one another. "Interdependence Day," they say, they actually giggle and kiss, take a rare bath after all. Intimacy builds up by its nature. One under the other—"Let me—" and then, then, after, staying power. Flash paper. Interrelation. They have some toys, vibrators and things, but Freak's underpants tend to wear out in one spot not from rubbing while Tango watches but *from Tango watching*.

Readiness is hardest of all to prove and maintain. When you costume with socks and kleenex, when necessity removes the outer leaves, when your audiences don't choose you, you better be ready to go. You better shell out for that original incident. If all that haunts, that follows is small: still. Be set to take that patch, the whole cracked grain. Radiant symmetry makes embrace possible, not just bowing out but bowing in. Utopia couldn't look like anything but itself, is what it couldn't look like, anything but what it is. In the very detailed dream there is nothing to fear anymore.

Bamboo?

Check.

Panda outfits?

Check, but this shirt is kind of more purple.

It won't show. Face paint?

Check. Raya had some left over from that last shoot.

Awesome. Clippers?

Check.

Okay, I think we're good. C'mere and let me do your face.

You do my black and I'll do your white—here.

The white is actually glow-in-the-dark.

Even better.

Local Gods

The National Pity Museum

You are to relive the pleasure of making, which endures,
        this object never meaning to you what it meant to me.
Artisanal pleasure of sitting still, moving
        only one small part of yourself, breaking to lick the thread.
Outside: hostility, howling, disorder, desert.
        Inside: the orderly tapestry of the way it happened, produced, used, destroyed.
I will be just like these spirits: mixed-use,
        vocal, awry, exclusionary.

Urban planning, you will give yourself a sickness. The edges are rough around you, the division still one of labor. When Sleep finds you, tell me what you think you were for. We made piles. We were moved by factors. Speak to me back through these.

I don't want to steal your story, but my story is the story of your destruction.
        I don't mind stealing your story, but don't want to have stolen it—to be that kind.
And now this story is the story of my destruction
        in which I keep nothing I've made
but wait here until Sleep comes for me.
        Tall Sleep, god, compulsion and obligation.

At the transformation table, materials permit you. Can Abundance excuse you? She asks for no help, constantly interrupts herself, heaped up and torn down by hands and machines—different hands, different machines, devotees. Demand and supply are easiest to imply. Hardest to implode. To implore: how divide any labor? The great demand that changes everything in its own time. Machines most people, handless, still picture.

Look at Abundance now, she comes adorned.
    You are to taste Her sweat.
She is about the house, Her sweeping furbelow,
    Her train in the dust of storefronts. Who that dust once was.

Her store in the Distillery is splendiferous, gorgeous, hard to believe, crammed, reclaimed—racks and their burdens burgeoning, augmented, barnacled, sleeves of one, bodice another, leather cuffed and riveted and printed, collars gathered and rickracked and appliquéd, laced, beaded, scrapped, redeemed. Like Frankenstein's monster in cobbled and highstepping drag, winsome and rigid. She is not like Sleep, but works from the center, saying "Repurposed" saying "Sustainable" materials draped and binned behind Her; many-armed, munificent, each arm folding or pinning, stretching or tucking, stitching, affixing, adding. Bobby pins with blobs of fur. Leather-lashed eyes. Apply these to your body, scratchy, restless, natural and synthetic, thought of and made in the building where once completely different people boiled and bottled and coiled and spoiled, shunted and formed, facted, faceless, facetless, falsely perfected.

Water up. We usurp weed gardens.
    Friends kayak through their toxic basements, salvaging.
In Providence, it's moving-out day aboveground.
    Belowground, the factory legacy leaches and releases.

Disallowed, they guard their lockouts against the whole night.
        Brick facades, once flush, blanken.
Someone shoots them for a design thesis
        whose pages I can turn myself, all in one room.
THIS WALL INTENTIONALLY LEFT BLANK.
        This occasion for revisionist history,
traditionally seeing desertion and emptiness
        with the eye of miserific vision:
I'll be dead, disused, indefinitely.
        It would be nice if after a certain time
I could be made public,
        transient, nonprofit, like a museum exhibit.

In the building, an inscription made for the Jing family hopes that "this vessel will be used by the sons of my sons." The building is a museum and the bowl is metal, one of those things that every museum feels it has to have.

The story of my destruction is hard to believe.
        At the market in Toronto it seems impossible, it seems for sale!
"In 1803, Governor Peter Hunter issued a proclamation that the land bounded by
Front, Jarvis, King and Church Streets be officially designated the 'Market Block.'"
        A woman feeds her son banana chips.
Sleep is tall; the floor cuts Her at the waist.
        A terrifying cornucopia spills painted fish, coffee beans, cheese, strawberries.
In this way Abundance is also represented.
        Peel back the mercantile vision.
"There are restaurants and stores," comes back like a sour penny.
        I'll still have been here, a story for no one to personally desire.
I'll have left my shape in "handmade originals,"
        skull games, findings, duck-feet bag, wool swatches, the slag of making.

A woman in a parka lifts the top off a cigarette-butt repository to see if there are any half-smoked. A beautiful sunny day she endures: how can I, how *dare* I, say she contrasts with anything.

More than the living, the spirits of the dead have been cliché and useful,
        like fishbone combs carding the sky, like big machines carding the sky.
We can no longer pacify them with tinsel wheels, street fireworks, burned-off hands.
        Not their homes but their places of work subjects of the past,
syrup accumulation and heavy pieces sliding past one another,
        cleaned, unaffordable and redistributed.

Who does the city let live, let tenant the lifelike factory like an insect, clockwork jewel, more colorful and smaller, the buzzing infested warehouse remembering someone else's grandfather-story, quoting the model-maker on fungi and orchids, the factory in clean miniature? This is starting to sound like a story about authenticity; if I can prove it's not, can I carefully pile junk on my back, bead up my eyes? The city lets me live for now. Scrounging my internet, decorating the holes in my clothes, intellect and artifice intersect, intercepted, a little while. Items made from beads and skin, in cases. The Ghost Dance returns things to the way they were before, but how far before? Sleep will let the sap into my neck too.

Are you wondering about what I'm doing?
        Which of its essential components did you predict?
Museums believe in their attempts to make order of profusion,
        return nothing to use, but are graceful.
Times that weren't graceful—don't love them.
        If you don't know them, don't misname them.
Ghost talks, ghost summit, easy targets:
        migration of the fashion children.
But all they're doing is moving,
        gathering blame like the trail of a gown,
Sleep-cultists facing Abundance-cultists
        rallying 'round their fires or stoicism,
backdrops, stages, architectural conscience.
        Erasure of all success from the earth's surface.

What would *you* like to sustain? Sleep asks, cool hand on my ardor. "Small circles of fire." The age of use appears to give way to the age of ornament appears to give way to the age of ease, the beatific vision—easier to make, easier to get. Fluff in the eye, crystal in the teeth, dirt going begging for cleanliness, lung-fiberglass, grease in the life line. As many as we could, as high, as fast. Now brightness feathers its nest; tops city ground with pungent, plumy leaves and heavy internal waters; takes the place of pride in the city, how it moves down the coil.

Like Sails

The difference between girders and beams
floods
the difference with lavender and yellow light
The differences between lavender and yellow light
deepen into the deep blue of blueprints

Streets and buildings empty of people but full of stone, garbage, animals, asphalt, cars, rats, pigeons, squirrels, sparrows, cockroaches, souvenirs, fleas, mice, lice, people, mites, lights, silverfish, Sleep.

Nice—daytime moon
Nice—yellow light cold-lidded, critical
Cars roll by sometimes with such a gentle purr

When I. was a girl he was already forming architectures, investigating homes. We go from room to room not thinking our path is also something made. A single family reserving home for itself. How much a family makes—not just in the money sense. Should homes be more or less like people or like factories. Recharged, a vision of building rubbing against his sky.

How high
How far
The plume of steam
Of bats
Of smoke
Like sails
The flight that harbors

Blueprints are blue because someone coated the paper with a solution of ferric ammonium citrate and potassium ferrocyanide. Strong light converts exposed areas to insoluble blue ferric ferrocyanide—Prussian Blue. Someone else washes the soluble chemicals off with water, leaving a light-stable print. Or, blueprints are blue because for almost a century blueprint was the only low-cost process for copying drawings. I. understands transformations that do nothing to change what's essential. Buildings—elevations—fill and lift. Hinges, paper feathers, reveal the turbulent peaceful truth about what's essential and there, like the present, billowing.

Inchmeal new old self grain
moth larva in the
cornmeal mouse turds along
the stove cool
back of the neck from the window.

Say "Vibrant" say "Eviction" say "Future." All of these stray straw men-dogs easy to blame or believe; say "Commerce" say "Profit" "Profit from" "Nonprofit" eat sauerkraut in "Punk houses." Bacterial welcome conjunction and fermentation. Say "Vibrant" again say "Thriving." Jars glow and cool. Worms wriggle red in dark newspaper. Changing weather balloons, silvery copy of Sleep who will float down and cover all of us, however vigorously we change, it can't be the reason; say "Thermal" "Solar" "Intestinal flora" "Graywater" campfires in our delicate structures, our giant catastrophic heaps.

Enormously expensive public sculpture made of
tongue-clickings and head-shakings
Plaster saints of money-luck in the windows of
botanicas ("Plants and Religious Goods")
A man reposed under the giant abstraction of
whatever that thing is called in a still
because it offers shade to him, his chair and book
in use that's living and resolute

Now black builds on black, dark gray on dark brown, flat disuse on iron echoes and shadows, high and wrought and die-cut, shrinking his presence. He got a late start. He follows a trail of instructions and short candles up past old dynamos and vaults, cavernous, massive, flickering, looming, to where his surprise lover sits, to scale, in the lighted center of the floor.

Take notice of the windows.
Take more. Not empty.
Empty of value.
Thrilling with fear of passionate arson.
A rag-musty assemblage.
A busy, temporary kitchen.
A declaration of grandeur.
Plaster dust settles in the shape of A) a permit / B) permission.
It's when he tries to uncramp, to louver, he feels just how down his arms have been.

Toronto, ON & Providence, RI · 2010

Number and Gender: Tango in Paris

The one to be neither pitied nor reviled, yet, progresses white as a cat. Trappings exert a strange draw. Fend off, stop. An orange sign reports. There are people in this view, but all of them are busy. The first white glimpse, faint rustle, hits.

Tango expected France without realizing, that's to say opening, expectation to see what was inside. More faces. Second sighting: Tango crooking an arm, drawing a bead on one behind its window. Notebook frill out and pin, dummy ending at the neck. Shape and voice a man: "C'est bien, c'est joli, c'est charmant." Dress is feminine. Drawing is masculine. Looks after him, dogged by period satin, static.

Parisian dust the color of a wedding. Gare de l'Est dead ahead and just past. One of the two boules courts still has a sign: "Réservée pour l'Association de Boules Lyon." Inside each fence an inner fence of men on that dust, or separated from it by cardboard, or from the dress-colored sky by blanket shelter. Sitting up, asleep, or absent. Or entirely given without being acknowledged, except for the man next to each man's spot who watches his sneakers until his return to the ring. Which no question appears to enter.

Perfect balance between spectre and spectre. Every time Tango whirls another dress has merged with its reflection. Could be a cat, a boarding call, piece blowing, receipt. Butt against lamppost in a half-tree pose. Green water has lost its savor. The bridges become mechanical by turning into fences, the lack of regard is total, Tango gets up, retracts, continues. An ellipse in gender within the numbered city.

Place Pigalle by accident, out of hand. Automatic feel in the other side of a pocket. Thin, harassed-looking woman turns abruptly through a doorway toothed with pictures of masturbating women, says, "Bonjour," to its keeper, strides forward and in with a grip on her bag. The lovers tried once for solidarity's sake to get in with the sex workers' union, but didn't qualify. Already Tango's passed the Communist Party Headquarters in France, not large, postered with a brown-skinned girl holding a sign: "Mon Pays Est Ici." Just one here, one *here* at a time.

The turn into funereal territory comes on like a lurch. Arrangements, floral and stone, chance to make statements about the dead above their crumbling houses. Thin striped sides curl in shade and sun. At footsteps, lean out from rotten leather and photo plaque. Chair for the dead, the wearers of gowns, the living. Dwellers in white and wrought iron. The ones who knew what they were there for: to die young or for some female reason. A related yearning Tango thought was dead.

Reverent. Retrograde. The hill practically climbs itself: there are people here, but none of them are simple. Bins of clothes pick over, unfolding, holding up, everything must go by individual hurries. To wear throughout, celebrating only the bargain, possibly the fit. To unresist, become one of the moved again, who isn't fluid, who doesn't elude. Pinned into satin. A sound is missing. A laziness. Expectation of faces. Brown or veiled ... veiled.

It's that hour. The pretty girl machine is turned up high outside the Quick hamburger chain. "I want the dresses to stop reflecting on me, following their own reflections into me, coming to me the way my name did." Having looked at graves: "I've never heard of any of these people. But I want people to have heard of me. Us, I mean. Of us." Number is far away. The poor, the dead, the named.

Barn Door

Home localizes under,
briefly swirls together,
feelings of animal dread.
The plane trees are still trees
grayed out by night vision,
ghosts of possible size,
girthy or dusty, stunted,
fully leafed out, or haunted.

Home-feeling meaning safety
loves the auction ring,
old-fashioned and unthinking
animals after they leave it—

Too late, the barn door opens.
It turns out this is false,
human, split wood, and worse.

Q: Where are you going?
A: Out to be threatened,
leaving me split by shame,
locked in the barn with shades
of chances to protect you
mooing, yawing around me.
Hindsight. Dust. Definition
one face of a vocation.

Safe to be tattooed, hairy.
Safe to be gay, fat, shy.
A sip freshens the poison
it is to be told, "Be someone
else," the taste, the someone
you are timbered in you,
femmy and slimly dressed,
a bowl too full to empty.

Keep the location secret.
Keep home moving and brief.
The lure of beam and lintel
rises above an arm:
pine tree and moon tattoo
bouncing to sissy bounce,
having said or failed
to say what I have sold.

To overlap themselves,
femmy boys say, "Yes, and..."
improvisational,
not binary, but present.
The sideyard opens, strung
and silted up with lights,
invitation to enter
unconfined to the owner.

The human in the barn
hears the night fill with sound.
Learning makes me sick,
dreading the harm that comes
to recreate the picnic
along the hot crack margin.
Yes, and part of the city.
Yes, and safety, rumpus,
hindsight, and stolen horses.

Places in Math

Places in Math

Darkness is a substance, thick substance that comes between. Brightness is absence. Don't you know a creation story when you hear one?

There's a lot of dough here. There's a lot to involve. There's a lot at this address, an address up for sale. There's a surface mark, an orange mark. Adjacent, it changes value. There's a trick to it. There's a lot of diversity here, a job lot of resentment. A bright blot on darkness changes the tape. There's the rate at which the first posts are driven.

Shadows collect by number in the basement, at the downspout, stains. Mike T. and I were going to smear the new thresholds with tuna for purposes of elimination. Never got to them. Nothing stays purged. How far will the shadow and what will it shade? More growth? Potential? How long would it have taken us? And the value of our time?

The world, the insect city. The city that goes on, the late city. How long will it take the city before the city. Discount city: the sign lights up, lights glow, lights new: Discount City. The hoverers have found a winner to be brighter than the signs that say, "Stop Speculative Development," brighter than, "Olneyville needs affordable housing not luxury lofts," than, "¡Vivimos en este vecindario... pertenece a nosotros!"—brighter than bright.

Judgment is traveling toward migration at a rate but migration is always farther, always faster. Don't you know the river, almost a stream here, flows back on itself, curls over its shopping bags, its now possessions, packs its inevitable fish?

I saw banners streaming through the buildings. They had no place to live.

Lift off the angel roofs and insert the target statuettes, the sainted market. Plant lights to make people walking below the windows feel lonely. Some computations begin this way, with a pure softness, uncontaminated, breathing peacefully, untroubled, a speculative light.

No substitute for myth has heretofore been successful. Isolated efforts wheel around the towers like bats, tower the ads along the sides of buses. "These people couldn't walk to work." If you weren't one of these, you'd be home now.

There's a chair, there's a committee, panic forces a bubble in neon, housing air, rising. Reach the noonday clot people cross with strollers, not figures but people. Not signs but prefigurations.

The horror ghosts bring becomes tenuous. I saw other people pretending to be ghosts in order to enter the ghost preserve, with striped masks on, naturally. Posters hung to imitate habitat. In the stiff cornflowers, milkweed, false wheat bending, Queen Anne's stems with no air of vulnerability. No air at all.

Weird Math II

The beauty of marble over the beauty of succession. It is always as if heavy plunder were being spoken. Humans manacle each other to the lives they have, end to end. *The constraints of their former positions have unfortunately not allowed them the time to engage in the larger neighborhood.*

In a city of elimination it became necessary to bulldoze in order to save. Save on chips. Save on shoes. Save on a thirty-six-inch flat-screen, on leather couches, on bedroom sets, a short amount each month, each month longer and longer, a beautiful chainsaw of profit. To fill the house with blossoming sound. *It is certainly possible to grow an environment.*

Snapping at moments, answering questions they brought, *they came here with a respect for historic preservation and all the work that has been done to rehabilitate old structures*. Of shining stones, exclusive shining. Free publication in the bank lobby. The luxury issue.

The ghost story says they came here to better themselves. To have things. To do. Their kids to get part-time jobs, then to look fully good. The money the family thinks: there's money and then there's money that's far away. *In the end, they feel that it has simply discredited their name.*

Construction equates hope with speculation. With the overcast, *the existing community offers a rich fabric* up as a sacrifice. Offers coexistence up. Unzips the skyline upward, the city suit, casts it, sure that one succeeds the other. You don't grow an environment, it grows you. The math of apparitions states: if it appears, it is.

In an equation, I feel for them. In an inequality, I can't. As real as you can't see, examination hews closer first. To home. The city. The city's people. The armaments of luxury.

The letters, the levels, the vagueness, the wait. Everything set up to trap every day. Neither the *santos* nor the local product even make a dent in the prospect of remarkable living, offering up not offering *the ability to displace long-standing residents and bring about.* Everyone will still have to be somewhere, the dust of construction like pollen.

Safe as Houses

To belong to ownership: a twist too neat for inverse. The signs are going up everywhere. Looking around, we see them. Root birds'-nest fungi out of the aloe pot. Humble underpinnings, that desire has. Safe to own: the warp in your board, meld in your corner, to set your windows in. We should hang out our shingle: one kind of math or another done here. Every tenant's shingle should be out. The floor slopes from its hump. Time paid for by the wet trees that surround us explains the difference between "fewer" and "less." Properties. And less. Ownership links and sets through the city, puts on, shrugs off. Shuns and shuts out the bleared opposite.

Architecture supports each moment financially, moments that could be floating their independence over bridges. So say borrowed dwellers, tender more (weirdly, mathematically) to some moments than others. Not dream-logic but of the dream house, it proceeds. We can state about it. A waterdrop changes the shapes of everything nearby through reflection, not accuracy, just reflection. It isn't a true mirror or a rear-view or a mugger's mirror or the one James found on garbage night, big as me, with carven frame. All over the city in the waterdrop members of a privileged group rise early and snap at their husbands.

Praying at the shrine of safety to remove those who would harm me from the street. Meanwhile, before another of its faces, they are praying too. Kings of a little kingdom, where in the city is safe for you? The city where you are king may overlap a city where you are unsustained. City of your ghost style where you take on solidity. Hand over the keys to your safety, keep the city. Cover the city with your own body as the mud settles. Locked out try to find a more comfortable cramp to watch from. Noble-eyed resentment, suckhouse waste of skin, occupy the same the *exact* same space. Imagine swelling the other way, swearing no bird can land. The swerves you force in trying to alight. Moss bulges up around you. When you cross, rage crosses with you. Your torsos fill with sprung shadow.

The belief that ownership will save the city qualifies, comes under the heading, or falls. It's like saying that slow dreamlike boats piloted by mimes will, or dirty Valkyries on bikes. It's like going without saying to a city made of wood, PVC pipe and brick, bundles of hair that used to be rats and tax forms teetering on the lip of preservation. Sill of surface tension. City snapped at that moment. The key on rent day sears the hand, the office cools me by name, I hand over my math. Posters up for the New Urbanism, olive- and rust-colored friendly fire. Blades of fans that fall with a crash for no reason, or a rented wind. Apartment like paid silence; house, an alibi. Fewer lots, but less time.

Preserve Versus

attempting to break
away, corners were cornered

buildings with people
branded in them

woman pushing a stroller finds
herself turned back sharply
gel in her braids, her hair crying
baby, tightened scalp, hunger

storehouse of hunger, cornered
bewildered turn

indignation rising all
the while—that
moves against, moves
by careful, stiffens

treats a relic like its last illness
around which the tiers rise, whitely
beaming, rise

tension keeps itself

a small part of town
to jar
green metal going
up, a lid on it
heavily, buses forming
hairpin
sharp rise
to tap, to open

corner man
waiting

cramp—on the pavement
scale—you don't care
it's just a thing / the way
the relegations
the tight right now
coming into the bend

traffic gags

who, owning fixity,
limits to give it
corner the market

so tight
paint flakes

kinds of momentum: constriction,
accumulation, quiet, force

pen the historically so
accumulation
will strangle them

we're living on top
of each other here

wherever you go
displaces air
the powers tear you
apart from their questions
wherever you convert
water to usage

whipped neighborhood name
heeled dog
well

in submitting
brick rises anyway
argument leans, eats
into brick background
front paws of a shovel
empty and fill, one
rising shrinks the other
one spreading

lickspit light show
snake pit tighten
the air
conditioner
drips and drips

cornered, even air
chokes itself

in hot still
summers with no egress
occupancy

out to attract ghosts
convolvulus, the crossing plant
creates but doesn't preserve
entrances to hillsides

a sprig
locks in
locks work
both ways

permeabilities: chain
a man, linked, leashed
to his dog, stoop
vanishing / now

of him, think, the corner
thinks him for him, he
no longer crosses

the gag inches purposefully
the brand heats, swells

the limit that appears
to exercise
constricts like a throat

emptying one fills
the other justifying
the next
removal, apology

an infinite number of ghosts
may be assumed to fit
into a given space
given space

one with no substance can't sweat
can be any size
can be imagined

having made a box for the spirits to live
in I then invited them to come live in it
lined it with everything I was told

another building's southern
side exposed as seen
through bottle glass
as one might cry,
"Preserve us!" and
be answered

bolted to siding
plaque like amulet
preservation
token

living the life of that sweltering place
don't stop
it was made for you

Weird Math III

If anything is justifiable then anything is. Therefore a basic city of thinking changes hands, no changes, but thinking again. That the right choice rolls out a wide flat path that says do this *forgive me* because *because* applied to the future becomes the dangerous *therefore*. From cause to cry the danger birds' high spiral. One chases off another but not the one you think until they are too high to see. After which the city you've made dives in and out of the one you think, cormorant in a dirty river.

Absolute integer of your acts *and what else* buzzing up there like thousands of ships or ghosts of flies. Assurances around spires sharpened for a reason. If you believe equivalency you'll believe the fruits of it. Action as amulet, chains you vote for, leaf through the ledger of previous choices you believe is chained to you, recorded from the pocket all your deeds your leases your ownership extended to you as long as the fall birds shall incontinently happen. Name the storms that blow them to protect yourself.

Paper is wonderful ink is wonderful facts are recognizable facts are familiar paper is familiar the same barrier. Lesser evil shudders into a lower order when you think. Would you rather see the city roll down this side or that of the *thankless task*, the hill. Work to see uppermost in succession. Or at once see. That which is not sound in the timber is not sound in the fall.

Justification rolls over making over injury injuring everyone with need. Scrutiny crumbles its own so far *no* further the horns of wind blowing at dawn through *no* an alarm. Have I kept the public domain waiting in the morning tangled room waking panic, justification peeling in, do you deserve to have your motes free in the air. Can you explain the answers math does not admit.

Can salvation nest into the details can it be plucked like any devil from the burned house *be combed for it* from sanctuary *show me* point your pins into the roots of the nerves where it lives writing this, you too, attempting. No outer garment no other ledger-keeper. Because where do you go from relief that cancellation policy.

Postlude: Interdependence Day

James and I walk to Bell Street Park, where we were married. The cool fragrant evening a switch of my vision makes magical: yellow lights softening, dandelion heads, looking up under the conifers at James's suggestion. "That's where I saw the hawk couple having their snack." It's not because I'm personally content: I'm anxious, I'm bleeding, my mouth tastes like old coffee, I'm worried about my sisters, I have to pee... Nothing unmarred, nothing the way we already imagined it. Because of this, we have to imagine what has never been, can speak about it with hope instead of certainty.

NOTES

Sources:

The Providence Journal, Letters to the Editor, April 1, 2006.

George Herriman, quoted in *Krazy Kat: The Comic Art of George Herriman*, Patrick McDonnell, Karen O'Connell and Georgia Riley de Havenon. Harry N. Abrams, Inc., Publishers. New York 1986.

600 Receipts, Worth Their Weight in Gold, compiled by John Marquart of Lebanon, PA. John E. Potter and Company. Philadelphia 1867.

http://www.stlawrencemarket.com, official site of the St. Lawrence Market, Toronto, ON.

ACKNOWLEDGMENTS

Thanks to the following journals, anthologies and chapbook presses:

"Preserve Versus" appeared in *Cannibal.*
"Sugarbook: a misreading" and "A Far Cry" appeared in *Aufgabe*.
"Branded* living" appeared in *Women's Studies Quarterly.*
"Places in Math" appeared in *Coconut.*
"Local Gods: Like Sails" appeared in *The Planet Formerly Known as Earth*.

"Magical Urbanism," "Revolving Fund," "Weird Math I," "Weird Math II," "Weird Math III," "Safe as Houses" and "Interdependence Day" appeared in *A Sing Economy*, eds. Adam Golaski and Matthew Klane (Flim Forum Press).
"Local Gods: The National Pity Museum" appeared in *American Ghosts: Poets on Life after Industry*, ed. Lillien Waller (Stockport Flats).

"The Love of Freak Millways and Tango Wax" appeared as a chapbook, *The Love of Freak Millways and Tango Wax*, from Cy Gist Press in 2009.

Thanks to Caroline Noble Whitbeck, whose insightful comments got this book closer to what it wants to be; Mike Taylor, who performed part of "Number and Gender: Tango in Paris" on the Flaws album *Erect Nation;* Edie Fake and Dewayne Slightweight for their performances; and James for sharing it with me.

Special thanks to the cover artists: Tom Bubul, Cybele Collins, Jo Dery, Jungil Hong, Xander Marro, James McShane, and Mike Taylor.

BIOGRAPHICAL NOTE

Kate Schapira is the author of three other books of poetry: *TOWN* (Factory School, Heretical Texts, 2010), *The Bounty: Four Addresses* (Noemi Press, 2011) and *The Soft Place* (forthcoming from Horse Less Press in 2012). She's also the author of chapbooks from Flying Guillotine, Horse Less, Cy Gist and Rope-A-Dope Presses, from Portable Press at Yo-Yo Labs, and forthcoming from dancing girl press. She co-curates the Publicly Complex Reading Series in Providence, RI, where she writes, teaches, and works as a Writer in the Schools.

MEANDER SCAR Series

In the aftermath of Federal Disaster #1649, a flood along the Delaware River, Lori Anderson Moseman and Tom Moseman created the Stockport Flats Press to celebrate writers and artists whose creative buoyancy builds community. This series, *Meander Scar*, features wordsmiths who carve new pathways. The geological term, *flood meander scar*, refers to a river's "experimentation" as high water forges new flow patterns. Post-flood, the mainstream may never frequent these pathways; however, the record of such possibilities intensifies our awareness of how terrain changes. *Meander* conjures whimsy; *scar* suggests both injury and healing. Let's examine forms that enact such fullness.

Designed by Lori Anderson Moseman, this volume was created using Hoefler Text and Century Gothic, printed on 80lb paper by BookMobile. This on-demand edition has an initial printing of 110 copies.

MEANDER SCAR Titles

B_____ Meditations [1-52] by Matthew Klane (2008)
Building Codes by Belle Gironda (2009)
Elements by Deborah Poe (2010)
The Spectra by Fred Muratori (2011)
How We Saved the City by Kate Schapira (2012)
poem for the house by Katie Yates (2012)

Stockport **Flats** 2012

1120 East Martin Luther King Jr. Street Ithaca, NY 14850 (607) 272-1630

www.stockportflats.org